What Is Artificial Intelligence?

George Anthony Kulz

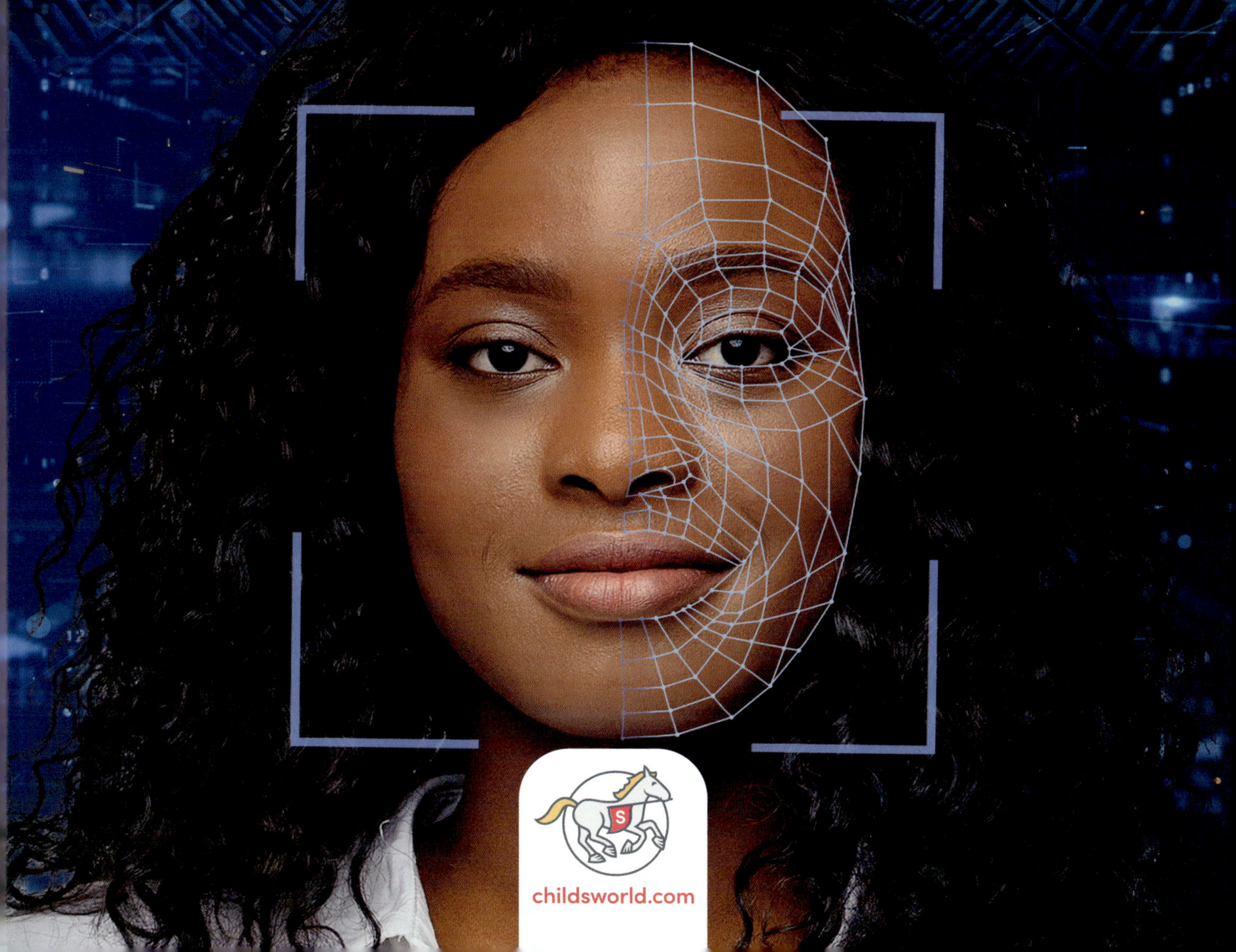

childsworld.com

Published by The Child's World®
800-599-READ • www.childsworld.com

Photography Credits
Photographs ©: Shutterstock Images, cover (person), cover (background), 1 (person), 1 (background), 8, 11, 13, 21; James Mattil/Shutterstock Images, 5; DC Studio/Shutterstock Images, 6; Ryan Sun/AP Images, 9; Joshua Sanderson Media/Shutterstock Images, 15; Phil Pasquini/Shutterstock Images, 16; Staff Sgt. Thomas Calvert/US Army/DVIDS, 19; Design elements from Tatiana Shepeleva/Shutterstock Images and Shutterstock Images

ISBN Information
9781503893849 (Reinforced Library Binding)
9781503894662 (Portable Document Format)
9781503895485 (Online Multi-user eBook)
9781503896307 (Electronic Publication)

LCCN 2024941405

Printed in the United States of America

ABOUT THE AUTHOR

George Anthony Kulz holds a master's degree in computer engineering. He is a member of the Society of Children's Book Writers and Illustrators. He writes for children and adults.

CONTENTS

CHAPTER ONE

A VISIT TO CES

Every year, the Consumer Trade Association holds a technology trade show called CES. Technology companies set up booths where they show off their latest products. People visit the booths to explore the cutting edge of technology. In 2024, some amazing products were on display at CES.

In one booth, a man sat in front of a screen that looked like a mirror. This device was called the Anura MagicMirror. A small green dot traced a circle around the man's face in the mirror. Once the dot finished drawing the circle, there was a pause. Information appeared on the screen. It showed the man's blood pressure, heart rate, and stress level. It also showed whether he was at risk of heart disease or **stroke**.

More than 130,000 people attended CES in 2024.

NVIDIA
TARAMPS
ELECTRONICS
Volkswagen
Connected
Community
I.D.
Polaroid
AXESS
I.D.
VR

The company that makes the Anura MagicMirror hopes to place it in clinic waiting rooms. That way, people could use it to check their health before seeing a medical professional.

Elsewhere, a man lay down on a special mattress called the T11 Pro Smart Mattress. As the man moved, the mattress changed its shape to support him. In this way, the mattress could help a person sleep more comfortably at night.

These products may seem different, but they have one thing in common. They are powered by artificial intelligence (AI). AI is the ability of computers to solve problems that normally require human intelligence. Computers using AI can **emulate** human intelligence. They appear to think and act as humans do.

AI allows the Anura MagicMirror to check a person's health. It does this by scanning her face. The AI looks at how the blood flows just beneath the face. The way the blood flows reflects parts of a person's health, such as her blood pressure and heart rate. The Anura MagicMirror's AI has studied blood flow in many people's faces. When a new person steps in front of the mirror, the AI can apply what it knows to study this person's face.

Some people's hips and shoulders get sore after sleeping on a mattress. Mattresses that adjust their own shape can help make sleeping more comfortable.

The T11 Pro Smart Mattress uses AI, too. The mattress gathers information such as heart rate and body position. It uses this information to tell how well a person sleeps. Over time, the mattress's AI learns how a person likes to sleep. It then adjusts the shape of the mattress to fit its owner.

People have been studying AI since the mid 1900s. Since then, AI has had a big impact on the world. People use AI to make familiar products such as mirrors and mattresses do new and amazing things. People also use AI to create new things, such as **chatbots** that can hold humanlike conversations. Experts expect AI to continue changing the world in the future.

GRILLING WITH AI

At CES 2024, the company Seergrills introduced Perfecta, a grill with AI features. Meat, fish, or chicken can be placed into the grill vertically, like bread into a toaster. The AI measures things such as the thickness of the meat. It then controls the burners on either side to cook the meat properly. The grill heats meat to more than 1,000 degrees Fahrenheit (540°C), fully cooking it in only 3 minutes. The grill's AI learns by accepting feedback each time it cooks something.

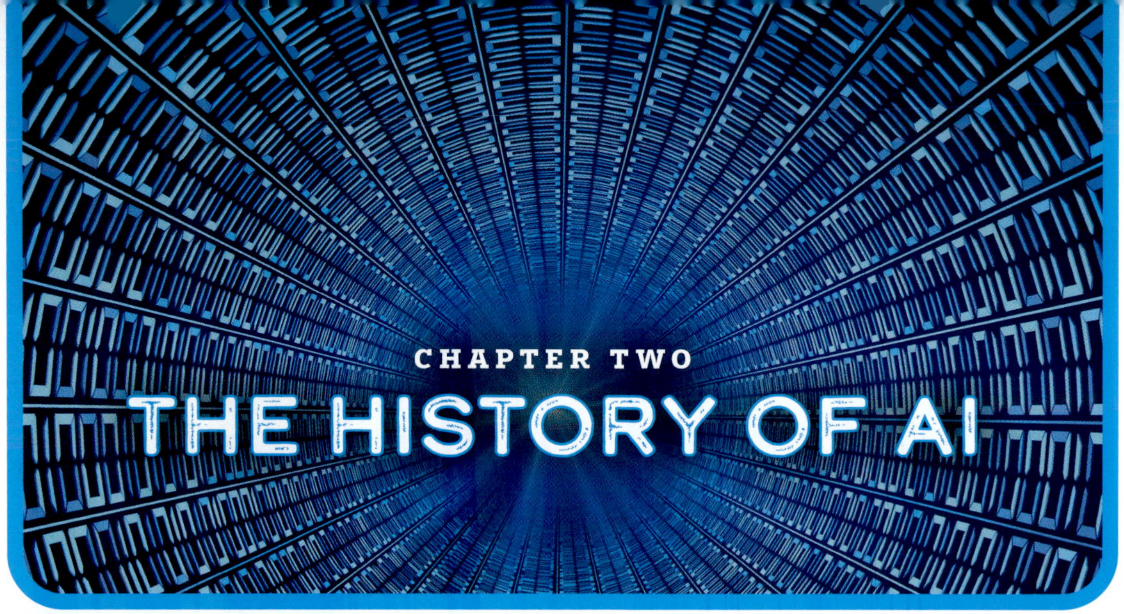

CHAPTER TWO

THE HISTORY OF AI

For thousands of years, humans have imagined creating intelligent beings. Jewish stories mention magical creatures called golems. In some stories, golems are clay statues that can be brought to life. The ancient Greeks wrote stories about Talos. Talos was a machine much like today's robots. It was said to protect the island of Crete.

The Greeks also designed automatons. Automatons are machines that can move on their own once a person has activated them. The Greeks designed mechanical birds, dancing dolls, and drinking figures. They were powered by steam, air, and water.

A cuckoo clock is an example of an automaton. When the clock strikes the hour, a small bird emerges from the device.

Modern computers were invented in the mid 1900s. In the late 1940s, Alan Turing was one of the first people to think about computers having AI. Turing was a pioneer in computer science. He thought that computers would someday solve problems and think as people could.

In 1955, John McCarthy was the first person to use the term *artificial intelligence*. He also came up with many important concepts related to AI. The following year, scientists wrote the first AI program. It was called the **Logic** Theorist. It could prove mathematical **theorems**. The scientists who created the Logic Theorist also created one of the first AI laboratories.

THE TURING TEST

Alan Turing came up with a test in 1950 that he called the imitation game. Today, it is known as the Turing test. In the test, a questioner asks questions to both a computer and a person. The questioner does not know which is the computer. The computer will try to trick the questioner into thinking it is the real person. If it succeeds, then the computer has the appearance of being intelligent.

Shakey inspired later robots that are able to explore their surroundings. For example, robot vacuums such as the Roomba explore a home's floors to clean up messes.

Two other important early uses of AI were ELIZA and Shakey. ELIZA was developed in the mid 1960s. It was a chatbot. It could respond to messages that people gave it. People who talked to it felt as if they were talking to a real person. Shakey was a robot created in the early 1970s. It could be told to do simple tasks such as pushing a block off a platform. After receiving a task, Shakey used AI to learn about its surroundings. It used that information to figure out how to complete its task.

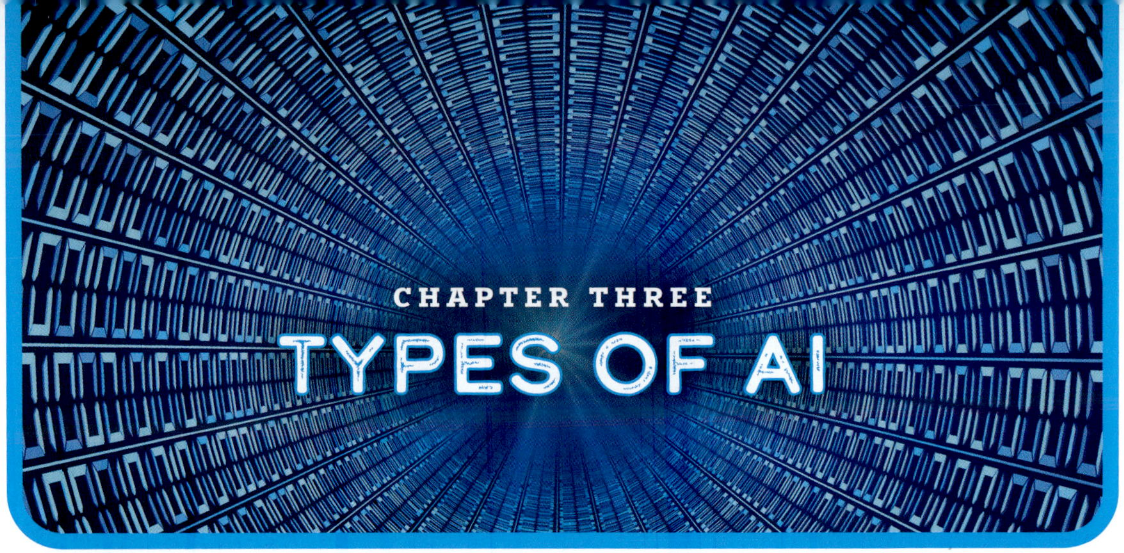

CHAPTER THREE

TYPES OF AI

Artificial intelligence can be divided into types based on how advanced it is. Narrow AI is the simplest type of AI. It is also the only type available today. Narrow AI is designed to do a specific job very well. For example, an AI handles the voice recognition software on phones. Narrow AI performs tasks faster and more accurately than humans. However, it is limited to what it is designed to do. It cannot reason or truly understand information.

Artificial general intelligence (AGI) and artificial superintelligence (ASI) are more advanced types of AI. AGI would be **self-aware**. It would perform tasks the way humans do. It would reason and understand. It could even have human emotions. ASI would have abilities far beyond any that humans have. It would be able to solve problems that people struggle to solve, such as finding cures for diseases, much faster than people ever could.

Phones with voice recognition features allow users to give the phone hands-free commands, such as telling it to open a map application.

The company Waymo produces self-driving cars that people can use as taxis. However, Waymo cars are only able to drive in limited situations.

Research is ongoing to achieve AGI. This kind of AI would make chatbots and self-driving cars much more powerful tools. For example, a self-driving car with AGI would be able to drive in all situations without human control. However, there is still a lot of work to do before people create AGI.

There are a variety of fields within AI. Machine learning is an important field. Machine learning is the ability of computers to learn in a way that resembles how people learn. Computers can find patterns in very large amounts of **data**. These patterns help the computers see relationships within the data.

Some fields of AI contain smaller subfields. For example, deep learning is a subfield of machine learning. The way deep learning works is inspired by the human brain.

Fields of AI can overlap with other fields. For example, computer vision is a field of AI that often overlaps with machine learning. Computer vision allows computers to process visual data such as images and videos. Computers can use this information to learn things about the world around them. For example, self-driving cars use computer vision to avoid obstacles.

Natural language processing (NLP) is another field of AI that often overlaps with machine learning. This kind of AI helps computers interpret and use human language. Chatbots using NLP can respond to people's messages in a humanlike manner.

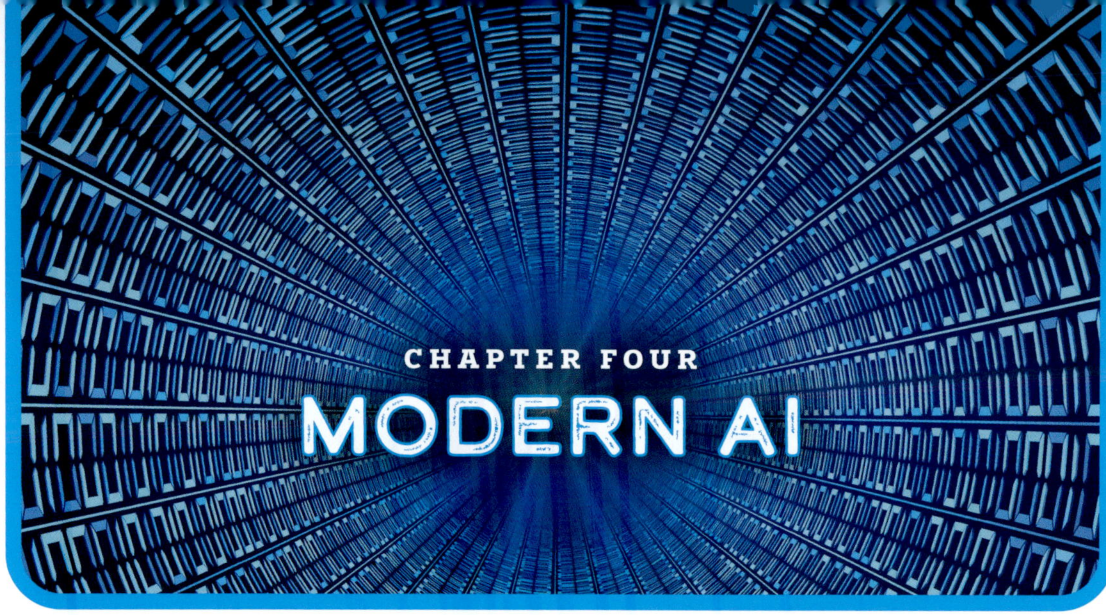

CHAPTER FOUR

MODERN AI

One of the most famous examples of AI is ChatGPT. ChatGPT is a chatbot. It uses deep learning and NLP to respond to questions and requests. It creates new material based on what it is asked to do and what it has already learned. AI that can create new things is called generative AI. Users of ChatGPT have used it to write articles, solve math problems, and even compose songs.

AI is also used in vehicles. Self-driving taxis give people rides from place to place. There are also **autonomous** vehicles that can fly. They can deliver things to people over long distances. They can also fly in places that are too dangerous or difficult for people. A Chinese company has even made a self-flying vehicle that carries passengers.

Drones are vehicles that fly but do not carry people. Some drones use AI to allow them to make flying decisions themselves.

AI technology has made people's lives easier. But AI has also come with many challenges. People have raised **ethical** questions concerning AI. For example, self-driving vehicles remove human error in driving. However, computer errors have caused accidents, too. People wonder about who is at fault in these accidents.

Some people fear AI. They worry that as AI becomes more advanced, it may take over jobs that humans normally do. People also worry about how AI affects their privacy. They are afraid that companies use AI to collect their personal information.

AI is going to become more advanced over time. It has the potential to make people's lives better. But for this to happen, people need to be careful when creating and using AI. If AI is not used responsibly, it could have negative effects.

RESPONSIBLE DEVELOPMENT OF AI

In 2023, President Joe Biden announced eight guidelines concerning AI in the United States. These guidelines directed how the government and US companies should act in response to the development of AI. The goal of the guidelines was to make sure that the United States enjoyed the benefits of AI and reduced its negative effects.

PRESIDENT BIDEN'S EIGHT AI GUIDELINES

- AI must be safe and secure.
- The US government must support AI development.
- Workers whose jobs are affected by AI must be supported.
- AI must not be used to deny **civil rights** to people.
- Consumers who use or buy AI products must be protected.
- AI must not illegally invade people's privacy.
- The US government must use AI properly.
- The US government must lead other nations in developing safe AI.

An executive order is a document signed by presidents to issue directions that have the force of law. In 2023, President Joe Biden issued eight AI guidelines in an executive order.

GLOSSARY

autonomous (aw-TAH-nuh-muss) Something is autonomous if it is able to act without outside control. Autonomous vehicles use AI to make driving decisions themselves.

chatbots (CHAT-bahtz) Chatbots are computer programs that can hold humanlike conversations. ELIZA and ChatGPT are two examples of chatbots.

civil rights (SIH-vuhl RITES) Civil rights are rights given to people by a government that protect people's freedom and equality in society.

data (DAY-tuh) Data is information collected for a purpose. Machine learning AI finds patterns in the data people give to it.

emulate (EM-yoo-layt) To emulate something is to try to be like it. An AI passes the Turing test if it successfully emulates a person.

ethical (EH-thih-kuhl) Something ethical is related to beliefs of what is right and wrong. People have raised many ethical questions about AI.

logic (LAH-jik) Logic is the science of reasoning. AI is capable of using logic.

self-aware (self-uh-WAYR) Something is self-aware if it has the ability to know or understand itself. Artificial general intelligence would be self-aware.

stroke (STROHK) A stroke is a medical emergency in which part of the brain loses its blood supply. The Anura MagicMirror uses AI to tell whether a person is at risk of a stroke.

theorems (THEE-uh-ruhmz) Theorems are statements that can be proved. AI can prove mathematical theorems.

FAST FACTS

- Artificial intelligence is the ability of computers to solve problems that normally require human intelligence.
- Alan Turing was a pioneer in computer science and AI. He proposed that someday a computer would be able to solve problems and think as people can.
- In 1956, scientists created the first AI program. It was called the Logic Theorist. It could prove mathematical theorems.
- The three types of artificial intelligence are narrow, general, and super AI. Narrow AI is the only type available today.
- Chatbots and autonomous vehicles are two examples of AI used in the world today.
- People have ethical concerns about AI. To reduce the negative effects of AI, these concerns will need to be addressed as AI development advances.

ONE STRIDE FURTHER

- What are some of the ways that AI is affecting the world today? Is it affecting you personally?
- Name one problem that you think AI could help solve. How could AI be used to solve it?
- What else can be done to make sure that people are protected from the negative effects of AI?

FIND OUT MORE

IN THE LIBRARY

Kelly, Christa. *Dangers of Artificial Intelligence.* Parker, CO: The Child's World, 2025.

Rathburn, Betsy. *Artificial Intelligence.* Minneapolis, MN: Bellwether, 2021.

Williams, Haley. *Artificial Intelligence in Everyday Life.* Parker, CO: The Child's World, 2025.

ON THE WEB

Visit our website for links about artificial intelligence:
childsworld.com/links

Note to Parents, Caregivers, Teachers, and Librarians: We routinely verify our web links to make sure they are safe and active sites. So encourage your readers to check them out!

INDEX